DISCOVERING THE CARIBBEAN
History, Politics, and Culture

WINDWARD ISLANDS

St. Lucia, St. Vincent and the Grenadines, Grenada, Martinique, & Dominica

DISCOVERING THE CARIBBEAN
History, Politics, and Culture

WINDWARD ISLANDS

St. Lucia, St. Vincent and the Grenadines, Grenada, Martinique, & Dominica

Tamra Orr

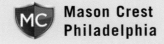

Mason Crest
Philadelphia

J
972.984
ORR
11/15
22.95

Mason Crest
450 Parkway Drive, Suite D
Broomall, PA 19008
www.masoncrest.com

©2016 by Mason Crest, an imprint of National Highlights, Inc.

Printed and bound in the United States of America.

CPSIA Compliance Information: Batch #DC2015.
For further information, contact Mason Crest at 1-866-MCP-Book.

First printing
1 3 5 7 9 8 6 4 2

Library of Congress Cataloging-in-Publication Data
on file at the Library of Congress

ISBN: 978-1-4222-3318-4 (hc)
ISBN: 978-1-4222-8635-7 (ebook)

Discovering the Caribbean: History, Politics, and Culture series ISBN: 978-1-4222-3307-8

DISCOVERING THE CARIBBEAN: History, Politics, and Culture

Bahamas	Cuba	Leeward Islands
Barbados	Dominican Republic	Puerto Rico
Caribbean Islands:	Haiti	Trinidad & Tobago
Facts & Figures	Jamaica	Windward Islands

TABLE OF CONTENTS

KEY ICONS TO LOOK FOR:

 Words to Understand: These words with their easy-to-understand definitions will increase the reader's understanding of the text, while building vocabulary skills.

 Sidebars: This boxed material within the main text allows readers to build knowledge, gain insights, explore possibilities, and broaden their perspectives by weaving together additional information to provide realistic and holistic perspectives.

 Research Projects: Readers are pointed toward areas of further inquiry connected to each chapter. Suggestions are provided for projects that encourage deeper research and analysis.

 Text-Dependent Questions: These questions send the reader back to the text for more careful attention to the evidence presented there.

 Series Glossary of Key Terms: This back-of-the book glossary contains terminology used throughout this series. Words found here increase the reader's ability to read and comprehend higher-level books and articles in this field.

Discovering the Caribbean

James D. Henderson

THE CARIBBEAN REGION is a lovely, ethnically diverse part of tropical America. It is at once a sea, rivaling the Mediterranean in size; and it is islands, dozens of them, stretching along the sea's northern and eastern edges. Waters of the Caribbean Sea bathe the eastern shores of Central America's seven nations, as well as those of the South American countries Colombia, Venezuela, and Guyana. The Caribbean islands rise, like a string of pearls, from its warm azure waters. Their sandy beaches, swaying palm trees, and balmy weather give them the aspect of tropical paradises, intoxicating places where time seems to stop.

But it is the people of the Caribbean region who make it a unique place. In their ethnic diversity they reflect their homeland's character as a crossroads of the world for more than five centuries. Africa's imprint is most visible in peoples of the Caribbean, but so too is that of Europe. South and East Asian strains enrich the Caribbean ethnic mosaic as well. Some islanders reveal traces of the region's first inhabitants, the Carib and Taino Indians, who flourished there when Columbus appeared among them in 1492.

Though its sparkling waters and inviting beaches beckon tourists from around the globe, the Caribbean islands provide a significant portion of the world's sugar, bananas, coffee, cacao, and natural fibers. They are strategically important also, for they guard the Panama Canal's eastern approaches.

The Caribbean possesses a cultural diversity rivaling the ethnic kaleidoscope that is its human population. Though its dominant culture is Latin American, defined by languages and customs bequeathed it by Spain and France, significant parts of the Caribbean bear the cultural imprint of

A pleasant beach on one of the Windward Islands.

Northwestern Europe: Denmark, the Netherlands, and most significantly, Britain.

So welcome to the Caribbean! These lavishly illustrated books survey the human and physical geography of the Caribbean, along with its economic and historical development. Geared to the needs of students and teachers, each of the eleven volumes in the series contains a glossary of terms, a chronology, and ideas for class reports. And each volume contains a recipe section featuring tasty, easy-to-prepare dishes popular in the countries dealt with. Each volume is indexed, and contains a bibliography featuring web sources for further information.

Whether old or young, readers of the eleven-volume series DISCOVERING THE CARIBBEAN will come away with a new appreciation of this tropical sea, its jewel-like islands, and its fascinating and friendly people!

(Opposite) A view of Curaçao, an island to the west of the others in the Windward group. It is located 35 miles (56 km) north of Venezuela. (Right) A waterfall cascades over mineral-encrusted rocks tinted yellow and green in Diamond Botanical Gardens, St. Lucia.

1 JEWELS OF THE OCEAN

SCATTERED ACROSS THE deep blue of the Caribbean Sea are the lovely Windward Islands: St. Lucia, St. Vincent and the Grenadines, Grenada, Martinique, and Dominica. Located in the southern group of the *Lesser Antilles* in the West Indies, these islands curve southward toward Venezuela and Trinidad and Tobago, covering over 300 miles (483 kilometers) of ocean. To the north are the Leeward Islands, which curve northward toward the British Virgin Islands.

While the islands of the Windward chain have many things in common, they also have intriguing differences. They vary greatly in size, as well as in the quality of *infrastructure* and the degree of European influence. Some islands have a distinct English air or a French flavor, while others are a charming blend of African, English, French, and *Creole*.

Visitors come from all over the world to vacation on the Windward Islands. With their warm, sunny weather, modern hotels and restaurants, and beaches that range from black volcanic sand to brilliant white, it is little wonder that the islands keep drawing tourists in ever-growing numbers.

EXPLORING THE ISLANDS

At the northernmost point of this island chain is Dominica. As "the Nature Island of the Caribbean," Dominica is the most mountainous, with four of its giant peaks measuring over 4,000 feet (1,220 meters). In the northern region is Morne Diablotin, the tallest mountain of the Windward Islands at 4,747 feet (1,447 meters). Another chain of seven mountains works its way down the

Words to Understand in This Chapter

Creole—a person of mixed black and French descent who speaks a dialect of French; also, the West Indian culture of such people.
fauna—animal life.
flora—plant life.
infrastructure—the system of public works of a country, including roads, railroads, and utilities.
Lesser Antilles—the name for a group of small islands in the Caribbean Sea that includes the Windward Islands.
mangrove—tropical trees that send out many twisting roots.
machineel—a tree native to the Windward Islands whose fruit, leaves, and sap are all poisonous.
trade winds—prevailing tropical winds that blow constantly from the same direction.

island from the center to the south.

Dominica has many deep and narrow river valleys, spectacular waterfalls, and four cold freshwater lakes. The island is also home to Boiling Lake, the second-largest thermally active lake in the entire world. With its large supply of water, replenished by the abundant rainfall of the Caribbean climate, Dominica has an incredible amount of vegetation. In fact, well over half of the island is covered in plants, trees, and flowers. It is a lush, rich island with extensive forests and an incredible natural park system.

The largest of the Windward Islands is Martinique, "the Pearl of the Antilles." Martinique is a highly developed island with a uniquely French flavor. Like Dominica, it is a lush, green island with rain forests, tropical plants, and trees. Tourists enjoy Martinique's simple beauty, but they also appreciate its modern hotels and restaurants. The mountains are

Grand Etang Forest Reserve and National Park protects a large tract of virgin rain forest in Grenada.

Quick Facts: Geography of the Windward Islands

Location: the Caribbean, between the Caribbean Sea and the North Atlantic Ocean; north of Trinidad and Tobago

Area:
St. Lucia: 238 square miles (616 sq km)
St. Vincent and the Grenadines[1]: 150 square miles (389 sq km)
Grenada: 133 square miles (344 sq km)
Martinique: 425 square miles (1,100 sq km)
Dominica: 291 square miles (754 sq km)
Terrain: volcanic and mountainous; St. Lucia also has some broad, fertile valleys.

Climate: tropical, moderated by northeast trade winds; all islands have a dry season (January–April), followed by a wet season four to seven months long, depending on the island. Hurricanes are common during the wet season

Elevation extremes:
lowest point—Caribbean Sea, 0 feet
highest point—Morne Diablatin, Dominica, 4,747 feet (1,447 meters)
Natural hazards: hurricanes, volcanoes; Dominica and Martinique experience flash floods

[1] Saint Vincent, 133 square miles (344 sq km)
Source: Adapted from CIA World Factbook 2015.

also a big attraction. Especially popular is Mount Pelée, a volcano that erupted violently in 1902 and devastated the city of Saint-Pierre.

The most developed of the Windward Islands is St. Lucia, a haven for tourists. In the center of St. Lucia stands Mount Gimie, towering over the island at 3,117 feet (950 meters). Gros Piton and Petit Piton, twin volcanic cones, lie in the southwest section of the island. Like the other Windward Islands, St. Lucia is green and fertile, and because it has changed hands between European powers more than a dozen times, it has a fascinating history.

The small island group called St. Vincent and the Grenadines is the least developed and poorest in the Windward chain. One of St. Vincent's most famous landmarks is Soufrière, an active volcano. Compared with the other islands, St. Vincent and the Grenadines don't receive many tourists. However, many sailors love the Grenadines, a chain of 30 small islands stretching over 80 miles (129 km) between St. Vincent and Grenada. Only a few of the small islands are inhabited. Bequia, one of the inhabited islands, measures only five by two miles (8 by 3 km), yet it is home to about 4,500 people and a great shopping place for sailors on the go. A few of the uninhabited islands are so small that some might consider them mere sandbars.

At the southernmost point of the island chain is Grenada, nicknamed "the spice island of the Caribbean" because it produces many different spices for the rest of the world. Life on Grenada is easygoing and casual. Visitors often stay there at night while exploring the Grenadines during the daytime. The island is developing steadily, and residents hope to make it as big a tourist attraction as St. Lucia. Unlike the other islands, which all have above-ground volcanic *vents*, Grenada has an underwater volcano that can be seen only from the air.

THE WEATHER REPORT

Because the Windward Islands lie within the Tropics, they enjoy lots of sun and warm temperatures, but the steady northeast *trade winds* keep the air comfortable. The average temperature on the islands is a pleasant 77° Fahrenheit (25° Celsius), with highs not usually above 90°F (32°C) and lows rarely below 55°F (13°C). Even the ocean stays warm; year-round the water averages a balmy 80°F (27°C)—just right for swimming.

Though people in the Windward Islands can appreciate the weather, they must also watch it carefully. Hurricanes—strong storms that develop over tropical waters—are a real problem for most of these islands. The hurricane season lasts from June through November, with the biggest storms usually arriving from mid-August to mid-October. One of the most devastating hurricanes, Hurricane David, hit the islands in August 1979, sweeping through Dominica with wind gusts of more than 150 miles (241 km) per hour. Twenty-two people were killed, and 75 percent of the island's population was left homeless. In recent years, other hurricanes have come close enough to do damage, but not on the scale of Hurricane David.

PLANTS AND ANIMALS

One of the great treasures of the Windward Islands is the lushness of their greenery. Blooming plants and trees adorn the landscape with a breathtaking smattering of color. Fruit trees produce delicious food, and rain forests, which are common to the islands, offer many other resources.

In Dominica, the Morne Trois Pitons National Park is a 17,000-acre (6,883 hectare) rain forest reserve so amazing that it is often referred to as a living museum. It is the oldest rain forest in the Caribbean. Dominica features more than 1,000 species of flowering plants, including 74 varieties of orchids and 200 kinds of ferns. In fact, more than a quarter of the island is protected as either a national park or a forest reserve.

The entire Windward Islands chain boasts incredible forests that feature the common *mangrove*, as well as a unique and dangerous tree called the *machineel*. This tree's leaves, sap, and fruit are all poisonous. Contact alone with the machineel can cause stinging and pain, and eating the fruit is fatal. Islanders advise tourists not even to stand under one of these trees in the rain because the water can be contaminated by running across the leaves. Forest rangers mark most of the trees with a sign or slash of red paint on the trunk.

Dominica's *fauna* is just as impressive as its *flora*. The island has the most diverse wildlife in the Windwards, with almost 200 different kinds of birds and a dozen species of bats. Visitors will sometimes spot iguanas reaching 3 feet (1 meter) in length, or cockroaches with antennae that protrude 4 inches (10 centimeters), or a blacksmith beetle so large that it makes a clanking noise when it scuttles across the ground.

The rest of the islands, however, have limited wildlife. They especially lack mammals, with few species besides the raccoon and the mongoose (both introduced by outsiders). Whales and dolphins can occasionally be sighted from the coasts. Reptiles and amphibians, such as tree frogs, snakes, geckos, and iguanas, are more common. There is only one species of poisonous snake, the fer-de-lance snake, which lives on Martinique. Birds of all kinds populate the islands, including the endangered sisserou parrot, the purple-throated hummingbird, the mangrove cuckoo, and the frigate bird, whose wingspan reaches 6 feet (2 meters).

TEXT-DEPENDENT QUESTIONS

1. What is Boiling Lake? On what island is it located?
2. Which of the Windward Islands is nicknamed the "spice island of the Caribbean?"

(Opposite) Workers harvest cocoa beans on a plantation in Grenada, 1934. The island remained a British possession until 1974. (Right) Old cannons still look out to sea in this fort from the colonial period. European nations such as Spain, France, Great Britain, and the Netherlands fought over the Windward Islands from the 17th through the 19th centuries.

2 A History of Struggles

TODAY, THE WINDWARD ISLANDS are distinct, independent countries (or, in the case of Martinique, an overseas department of France); they are not connected with one another politically. While the islands we know today as St. Lucia, St. Vincent and the Grenadines, Grenada, Martinique, and Dominica all have their own unique history, to a great extent they developed along a common path. And it was a path filled with struggle.

Indigenous Peoples

Perhaps as early as 300 BCE, a group of Amerindians known as the Arawaks began migrating from northern South America to the islands of the Lesser Antilles chain. Eventually they would settle islands as far north as the Bahamas. Generally peaceful, the Arawaks farmed, fished, and lived in small villages.

About 1,000 years after the Arawaks first settled the Windward Islands, another indigenous group from the South American jungles of the Amazon began moving into the Caribbean islands. These natives, the Caribs (from which the word Caribbean is derived), were quite different from the earlier settlers. They were fearsome warriors, and they practiced cannibalism.

By the time Europeans first arrived in the West Indies at the end of the 15th century, the Caribs had driven the more docile Arawaks out of the Windward Islands.

THE ARRIVAL OF THE EUROPEANS

During his first voyage to the so-called New World in 1492, Christopher Columbus did not sail near the Windward Islands. Instead, he and his crew spent about three months exploring the Bahamas and the Greater Antilles in the northern Caribbean. When he returned in 1493, however, Columbus did sight Dominica, and in later expeditions he would find other islands in the Windward chain: Grenada (which the admiral dubbed "Concepción) and

Words to Understand in This Chapter

privateer—a person authorized by his government to engage in acts of piracy against the ships of enemy nations during a time of war.
sanctuary—a place of refuge or safety.

Christopher Columbus spotted and named several of the Windward Islands during his third voyage across the Atlantic in 1498. However, during the early years of the 16th century Spanish manpower was needed to conquer and control the rich civilizations of Mexico, Peru, and Central America, and to administer settlements on larger Caribbean islands such as Hispaniola, Cuba, and Puerto Rico. As a result, Spain never really became involved with planting colonies on the Windward Islands.

perhaps St. Vincent in 1498; Martinique in 1502. But early Spanish interests in the West Indies lay mainly with the larger islands of the Greater Antilles, including Hispaniola and Cuba, and a little later with Mexico. As a result, the Spanish largely ignored the Windward Islands, though some Amerindians were taken as slaves to work in mines or on plantations elsewhere.

Indeed, for more than a century after the first European contact, the Windward Islands were mostly overlooked by the European powers. In the mid-17th century, however, the French, British, and Dutch began to colonize

Pierre Belain d'Esnambuc (1585–1636) came to the West Indies hoping to gain riches as a privateer. Instead, he became the leader of French settlements in the Caribbean. In 1525 he established a settlement on St. Kitts, one of the Leeward Islands. From that base he explored several other islands, and ultimately started a new French colony on Martinique in 1635.

these islands. And over the course of the next century and a half, they fought bitterly among each other—and with the native Caribs—for control.

CENTURIES OF STRUGGLE

In 1635, Pierre Belain d'Esnambuc, a French *privateer*, arrived on Martinique to begin colonizing the island for his country. Belain struck an agreement with the Caribs living on the island: he would give them the western half if they permitted the French to settle the eastern half. By 1660, however, the French had completely abandoned their promises. They killed some of the Caribs and forced the others off the island.

To work Martinique's expanding sugarcane plantations, the French imported slaves from Africa. By the 18th century, these plantations were so successful that Martinique was considered one of France's most popular colonies.

As on Martinique, on Grenada relations between the Caribs and the French (who arrived in 1650) were initially fairly cordial. In fact, the Caribs invited the French to settle on the island in exchange for trade goods such as metal axes and knives, mirrors, and alcohol. Within four years, however, the Caribs

An 18th-century British drawing of Port Royal, the main port of Martinique. France and Great Britain often fought over the Windward Islands, and possession of a number of small islands changed hands several times.

had changed their minds about the presence of the French, and a struggle for control of the island broke out. Grenada's Caribs called on neighboring tribes from St. Vincent and Dominica for support; French settlers from Martinique arrived to join the fight in support of their countrymen. In the end, the Amerindians' bows and arrows were no match for the Europeans' firearms. Those Caribs who escaped fled north to Dominica or St. Vincent, but many were killed in battle or jumped off cliffs to their deaths in front of the advancing French.

In 1762, it was the French who were routed on Grenada, by the British. At the time, the two nations were engaged in a wide-ranging struggle known as the Seven Years' War. In 1763, at the war's conclusion, France ceded the island to its rival. But less than two decades later, while England was occupied in North America fighting the American Revolution, France took the island back. The French ruled from 1779 until 1783, when they returned Grenada to the British. More troubles came for the British in 1795 and 1796, when they had to fight to put down a native uprising.

The early history of St. Vincent is remarkably similar. The French established the island's first European settlement, in 1719. The island became a British possession in 1763 and was occupied by the French from 1779 until 1783, whereupon it was returned to the British. A Carib uprising broke out in 1795. After the uprising was suppressed, the British deported the surviving natives.

But St. Vincent was also the scene of a unique development. In 1675, a ship full of African slaves was shipwrecked on the island. The surviving Africans blended with the native Caribs, creating a new group called the Black Caribs. For a long time St. Vincent was also a *sanctuary* for Caribs from other islands who were fleeing from the Europeans.

On St. Lucia, the native Caribs fiercely resisted both the British and the French until 1660, when they agreed to a treaty with the latter. Over the course of the next century and a half, however, the island changed hands 14 times between the French and the British. Finally, in 1814, the French ceded control of St. Lucia to Great Britain.

The last of the Windward Islands to be settled by Europeans was Dominica. The native Caribs fought furiously against the invaders, but in the 18th century the French finally gained a foothold. Throughout the century, France and England battled for control. In 1783 France ceded Dominica to the English, and the island became a British colony in 1805.

Slavery in the Windward Islands

Both the French and the British imported large numbers of African slaves to work their plantations on the islands. By the time slavery was abolished—in the British colonies in 1834, on the French island of Martinique in 1848—blacks made up a significant proportion of the populations of the Windward Islands. To varying degrees, mulattos—people of mixed black and white ancestry—came to be part of the racial makeup of the islands as well.

Ninety Seconds of Terror

On the morning of May 8, 1802, the residents of Saint-Pierre, the capital of the French overseas department of Martinique, were going about their business as usual. Saint-Pierre, a city of 38,000, enjoyed many of the modern conveniences available during the early years of the 20th century, such as electricity and telephones.

The city lay in the shadow of an active volcano, Mount Pelée, which for months had been rumbling and spewing smoke. Some people predicted that a major eruption was bound to come, but the residents of Saint-Pierre ignored the dire warnings.

At 8 A.M. on May 8, catastrophe struck. Pelée exploded with a force 40 times more powerful than the atomic bomb that would be dropped on the Japanese city of Hiroshima in 1945. Superheated gas, burning ash, and lava were sent more than 300 feet (92 meters) into the air. Lava raced down the side of the mountain toward Saint-Pierre at an astonishing 250 miles (402 km) per hour. The residents never had a chance. Within 90 seconds the entire city was destroyed, and all 38,000 people who had been casually going about their morning routines just minutes before were dead.

All except one, that is. Auguste Cyparis, the only survivor of the catastrophe, was in a jail cell, having been arrested the night before for public drunkenness. The thick walls of the jail saved him from the torrent of lava that swept over Saint-Pierre. He was found three days after the eruption, hungry but unharmed. Cyparis spent the rest of his life touring with P. T. Barnum's circus as the sole survivor of the 1902 Mount Pelée eruption.

INDEPENDENCE

After the Saint-Pierre catastrophe, the capital of Martinique was moved to Fort-de-France. Today, Martinique remains an overseas department of France.

This photograph of smoking Mount Pelée was taken in May 1902, a few days after the volcano erupted suddenly, destroying Saint-Pierre, the capital of Martinique, and killing some 38,000 people.

For the British-held Windward Islands, however, independence would come in the 1970s. Grenada was first, becoming an independent state within the British Commonwealth on February 7, 1974. Dominica became an independent republic in 1978. St. Lucia and St. Vincent and the Grenadines were granted independence in 1979.

TROUBLE ON GRENADA

Less than a decade after becoming independent, Grenada was the scene of a military coup and an American-led invasion. The trouble began on October 19, 1983, when a group of Communist Grenadian army officers led by

A U.S. military helicopter patrols over Grenada, November 1983. U.S. forces invaded the island on October 25, 1983, because of concerns that Cuba's Communist government had gained too much influence.

Deputy Prime Minister Bernard Coard seized control of the government. A few days later, the officers murdered the deposed prime minister, Maurice Bishop.

In Washington, the administration of President Ronald Reagan, a staunch anti-Communist, watched the developments on Grenada with concern. Technical advisers from Fidel Castro's Cuba were known to be in Grenada, and the administration did not want to take the chance that Grenada would join Cuba as the second Communist, anti-American nation in the Caribbean. In addition, some 1,000 Americans were living on the island, most of them students at St. George's School of Medicine. The administration expressed concern for the safety of these American citizens. In addition, the Organization of Eastern Caribbean States and Grenada's British governor-general, Sir Paul Scoon, formally appealed to the United States to intervene.

On the morning of October 25, just six days after the coup, 1,200 soldiers—including U.S. Marines, Army Rangers, Navy SEAL commandos, and troops from other Caribbean nations—invaded Grenada. Within a few days, the invasion force had swelled to 7,000 soldiers. The Grenadian army and several hundred Cubans fighting with them were quickly overwhelmed. Nineteen Americans died in the brief war, and 119 were wounded. Casualties for the Grenadians stood at 45 dead and 337 injured; 59 Cubans were killed and 25 wounded.

In 2004, Hurricane Ivan destroyed 90 percent of the homes and buildings on Grenada, including this Anglican church in St. George.

The coup leaders were ultimately captured, and all the American medical students returned home unharmed. Free elections were held on Grenada the following year.

TEXT-DEPENDENT QUESTIONS

1. What French privateer established the first European settlement on Martinique?
2. How many people were killed when Mount Pelée erupted in 1902?
3. Which of the Windward Islands was the first to gain independence?

(Opposite) Cocoa beans dry in the sun at historic Dougaldston Spice Estate near Gouyave, Grenada. (Right) A tourist enjoys the scenery from horseback. Tourism brings more money into the islands of the Windward group than any other industry.

3 Of Bananas, Nutmeg, and Tourists

LIKE THE ECONOMIES of other Caribbean islands, the economies of the Windward Islands have evolved over time. Most of the island populations once depended on sugarcane plantations for revenue, though that changed when Europe began cultivating its own sugar beets and the drop in demand for the islands' sugarcane forced factories to close down. Island life may seem easy, but having to depend heavily on imports for essentials like meat, grain, and equipment poses great challenges.

Bananas and Visitors

Bananas are an important export of the Windward Islands. Production and sales of this fruit have greatly affected the daily lives of many people since the 1950s. A variety of bananas are grown on the islands, including the big, bright-yellow cavendish and gro michel types; the small, sweet canary banana; and the plantain.

In Martinique, the largest of the Windward Islands, most of the meat, grain, and vegetables needed to fee the people must be imported. Thus the cost of the country's imports is much greater than the value of its exports. The island receives financial support from France to address this *imbalance*. Sugarcane production continues in only one factory, primarily as an ingredient in the production of rum. Today, like many Caribbean islands, Martinique depends on export revenues from bananas—shipped primarily to France—and tourism, which brings in more revenue than any other industry.

No island depends more on banana production than does St. Vincent. In fact, with bananas as almost its sole source of income, the island's economy is often at great risk. When tropical storms wipe out crops, as they did in 1994, 1995, 2002, and 2013, the economy suffers. St. Vincent's government has compensated for this problem by increasing efforts to build up the tourism industry, but the country only draws a modest 200,000 visitors each year.

Dominica is also highly focused on banana production. About 40 percent

Words to Understand in This Chapter

eco-tourists—tourists concerned with the environment.
imbalance—a lack of balance, as in proportion or distribution.

Quick Facts: Economy of the Windward Islands

	GDP	GDP per capita
Dominica	$1.015 billion (2013 est.)	$14,300 (2013 est.)
Grenada	$1.46 billion (2013 est.)	$13,800 (2013 est.)
Martinique	$10.7 billion (2012 est.)	$27,688 (2012 est.)
St. Lucia	$2.22 billion (2013 est.)	$13,100 (2013 est.)
St. Vincent / Grenadines	$1.335 billion (2013 est.)	$12,100 (2013 est.)

*GDP = the total value of goods and services produced in one year.

Sources: CIA World Factbook 2015; Institut national de la statistique et des études économiques (Martinique).

of Dominicans work on farms, and banana sales account for about one-fifth of the island's gross domestic product (GDP)—the total value of all goods and services produced in a year. The island does not draw large numbers of tourists because it has no international airport and its rugged coastline leaves hardly any room for beaches. Many Dominicans are content that their island has not become a tourist hotspot. They don't want the construction of hotels, restaurants, and casinos to destroy the natural beauty of the island. They do encourage *eco-tourists* to visit, however. And recently, the island has turned to soap production for income, in addition to developing its offshore financial industry.

St. Lucia knows well what can happen when the banana market suffers. Its banana sales have been declining since the 1990s due to competition from other countries in Latin America.

Like St. Vincent, St. Lucia is setting its sights on improving tourism on the island, focusing on constructing hotels, restaurants, and other attractions.

St. Lucia is also concentrating on the manufacturing sector and on creating small offshore financial businesses. In 2013, the government introduced a National Competitiveness and Productivity Council to help make St. Lucia more competitive economically with other Caribbean countries.

Grenada's economy depends on an entirely different product—spices. The tropical breezes carry the rich aroma of spices throughout the island. Grenada is, second only to Indonesia in the production and exportation of nutmeg. The spice is even represented on the country's national flag. Since it was first introduced to the island in 1863, nutmeg has played a large part in

The colorful Saturday market at St. George's Market Square, Grenada.

A banana plantation south of Marigot, St. Lucia. Banana production remains an important part of the economy for all of the Windward Islands.

the economy. It is made from the fruit of 60-foot-tall evergreen trees, which also produce the spice mace. Along with these spices, Grenada produces cinnamon, cloves, allspice, pimento, ginger, bay leaves, and vanilla. The spice industry was devastated by Hurricane Ivan in 2004, and Hurricane Emily in 2005. However, it has recovered, although money borrowed to rebuild the infrastructure has led to higher taxes. Like the other Windward Islands, Grenada is continuing to develop and promote its tourism industry.

TEXT-DEPENDENT QUESTIONS

1. What fruit is an important export crop for the Windward Islands?
2. On what agricultural product does Grenada's economy depend?

(Opposite) Canute Caliste, a painter from Grenada, shows off a picture in front of his studio in Carriacou. His paintings have been shown in galleries in Grenada, London, and New York. (Right) Colorfully costumed dancers participate in a Carnival celebration.

4 The Culture and People of the Windward Islands

THE PEOPLE OF the Windward Islands have much in common. For instance, blacks are the predominant race and the vast majority of the people are Roman Catholic. But once again, each island has a distinct identity shaped by its history and cultural background.

The Martinicans

Unlike most of the other Windward Islands, Martinique has a distinctly French flavor. The currency, cuisine, and fashions are all French; yet, because of the past blending of cultures, there is also a strong French-Indian Creole feeling to the people and the island. It can be heard in the music, tasted in the food, and observed in the customs. While French is the main language, many of Martinique's nearly 400,000 people also speak Creole, a combination of French and African words.

Popular foods are *baguettes*, *croissants*, and *feroce* (a mixture of avocado, hot pepper, and cod salad). A favorite island drink is ti-punch, a blend of rum, sugarcane syrup, and lime juice. Martinicans are proud of their bolero style of music and the **biguine**, an Afro-French dance. Another form of dance often appearing in annual carnivals and celebrations is the **zouk**, a sensual dance with a strong beat that has become popular all across Europe.

One of the most famous Martinicans was Aimé Césaire, a poet and former mayor of Port-de-France. During the 1930s, Césaire popularized the concept of **Négritude**, which emphasized the importance of black African achievements and culture. Césaire's ideas influenced the Black Consciousness movement of the 1970s, which had a significant impact on Latin America, the United States, and Africa.

Words to Understand in This Chapter

biguine—an island dance of French origin.
culinary—having to do with cooking.
emigration—the act of leaving a place or country to live elsewhere.
Négritude—a re-connection to African roots.
patois—a mixture of two or more languages.
regatta—organized series of boat races.
zouk—an island dance popular in Europe.

An ornate Catholic church on the island of Martinique. Most of the islanders are Roman Catholic.

Martinique's calendar is filled with holidays. On May 8, citizens remember the eruption of Mount Pelée with a live jazz concert and a candlelight procession. They also have an annual Mardi Gras festival, complete with music, dancing, and parades, plus several sporting events, such as the Tour de la Martinique, a weeklong bicycle race, and the Tour des Yoles Rondes, a weeklong sailboat race.

THE VINCENTIANS

Most of the roughly 120,000 residents of St. Vincent and the Grenadines are descendants of African slaves who were brought to the island to work on the plantations. Others are descendants of Caribs, English colonists, or East Indians. English is the main language, although some residents of a few of the inhabited Grenadines speak a French *patois*. Unemployment on St. Vincent is high and so is *emigration*, as many people decide to seek jobs elsewhere.

The Vincentians celebrate Vincy Mas or Carnival sometime between the end of June or early July. It is the main event of the year, featuring a month of calypso music competitions and dancing in the streets.

THE LUCIANS

On St. Lucia, home to an estimated 174,000 people in 2015, there is a visible blend of the French and the English. Even though England won final control of the island, the influence of the French culture has endured. English is the main language, and the island's educational, legal, and political structures are based on British models. However, the island's music, dance, and language have strong French influences

The renowned poet, playwright, and essayist Derek Walcott was born in St. Lucia in 1930. His works often examine the experiences of Caribbean islanders.

The restaurants in St. Lucia have received wide acclaim, winning gold medals in important *culinary* competitions. Cooks combine the island's produce—including papayas, pineapples, passion fruit, and coconuts—with the day's catch to create exotic dishes like callaloo soup, which is the national dish. The island's kitchens are also known for their curries and pepper pot stews.

St. Lucia is also home to two Nobel Prize winners: Sir W. Arthur Lewis, who won the Nobel Prize in economics in 1979, and poet and playwright Derek Walcott,

Quick Facts: The People of the Windward Islands

Population: 864,874 (total for all islands).

Ethnic groups: black or mixed black majority; minorities include Europeans, East Indians, Chinese, Carib Amerindians.

Population growth rate: 0.317%

Birth rate: 17.14 babies born / 1,000 population.

Death rate: 8.83 deaths / 1,000 population

Infant mortality rate: 13.78 deaths / 1,000 live births.

Life expectancy at birth: 72.88 years.

Total fertility rate: 2.01 children born per woman.

Religions: Roman Catholic, Anglican, other Protestant, Hindu, indigenous African.

Languages: English, French patois (Dominica, Grenada, St. Lucia, St. Vincent and the Grenadines); French, Creole patois (Martinique).

Literacy rate (age 15 and older who have attended school): between 90% (St. Lucia) and 96% (Grenada).

Unless otherwise noted, figures are averages of statistics for the Windward Islands.
Adapted from the CIA World Factbook 2015.

who won the Nobel Prize in literature in 1992.

The St. Lucians celebrate the anniversary of their independence on February 22. In December they celebrate their national day with sailboat races and parties. The biggest holiday, however, is Carnival, a pre-Lenten festival with parades, costumes, and music in the streets.

THE DOMINICANS

Dominica is the only island in the eastern Caribbean that still has a significant Amerindian population. About 2,500 of the island's 73,000 residents are Carib Indians; they live on the eastern coast. The island struggles economically and is often laboring under an unemployment rate of more than 20 percent. Street

A Carib weaver creates a basket on the Carib Indian Reserve, Dominica.

names are a jumbled combination of French and English, and a West Indian patois is commonly spoken. Unlike the other islands, Dominica is not interested in increasing its tourism industry, preferring to keep the island as unspoiled as possible.

Festivals include Carnival, also called Masquerade, in the days before Lent. Independence Day is celebrated in early November. Domfesta is a yearly festival of local arts, crafts, and performing arts held in the summer months.

THE GRENADIANS

The history of this island's name reveals much about the history of the island itself. The first inhabitants called it Camerhogne. Columbus arrived and renamed it Concepción; later it was called Mayo. Upon settling the island, the Spaniards named it Granada after a region in their homeland, and then the French translated this to La Grenade. When the British finally made the island a permanent settlement, they called it Grenada, the name by which the island continues to be known today.

The 110,000 residents of this island appear to be more interested in politics than are the citizens of the other Windward Islands. It is a favorite topic of conversation, and Grenadians are known for quizzing tourists about world politics and economics.

English is the main language, but a French patois has been more commonly spoken in recent years, and a sprinkling of Spanish words have entered the Grenandians' vocabulary. The Spanish additions are the result of Grenadians leaving the island to work in nearby Spanish-speaking countries like Cuba or Costa Rica and then returning with their newly learned foreign words.

Grenadians celebrate Carnival in August, and it includes three days of dancing in the streets of St. George, with parades, singing, and steel bands. There is also a sailing *regatta* in August, Independence Day in February, and Extempo, a performance where singers ad-lib on stage, in November.

TEXT-DEPENDENT QUESTIONS
1. What are two dance styles popular in Martinique?
2. About how many people live in St. Vincent and the Grenadines?
3. What is the main language of St. Lucia?

(Opposite) The landmark Pitons, twin volcanic peaks rising out of the cobalt-blue Caribbean, tower over the French colonial town of Soufrière, St. Lucia. (Right) A local bus carries tourists up a hill on St. Vincent.

5 A Tour of the Cities

BECAUSE THE WINDWARD ISLANDS are so small, there are very few cities on each of them. Many just have a capital city and some small villages scattered about the island.

Roseau

Dominica's capital, located on the southwestern coast, is Roseau. About a quarter of the island's entire population lives in this city, Dominica's only sizable town. Although it doesn't receive a lot of tourist traffic and can usually measure its rainfall in tens of feet rather than in inches, the city is still quite beautiful. Natives say there is always a rainbow somewhere nearby. Hurricane David destroyed much of the city in 1979, but it was rebuilt with the same old-style Creole houses replacing the originals.

Most of the activity in Roseau takes place in the Dawbiney Market Plaza, formerly know as the Old Market Square. It is hard to believe upon first glimpse that this cobbled square was once the site of slave trading and public executions. The city offers botanical gardens dating back to 1851, a public market, and ferries to the nearby islands of Martinique and Guadeloupe. In the east coast region are the eight Carib villages where the 2,000-plus descendants of the original Caribs still live. Keeping to tradition, these Caribs still specialize in building boats and weaving intricate brown, black, and white baskets.

MARTINIQUE'S CITIES

Fort-de-France, a chic, modern city, is the capital of Martinique. About one-third of the island's entire population lives there. It has a large bay that offers a wide view of the Caribbean Sea. Some consider it the most beautiful view in the West Indies. Fort-de-France is unlike any other city in the entire chain of islands. It has the latest fashions hanging in store windows, and restau-

Words to Understand in This Chapter

eclectic—chosen from various places or sources.
haute cuisine—fancy entrees and food items on a menu.
petroglyph—a carving or line drawing on rock, especially one made by prehistoric people.

rants feature true *haute cuisine*. Much of the activity in the city revolves around the Place de la Savane, the city's central park. Over a dozen acres in size, it features royal palms that reach 100 feet (31 meters) tall, helping to create a regal and tropical atmosphere. The city has many sites for visitors, including an archeological museum, an open-air market, and Fort Saint-Louis, which dates back to 1638.

Other cities on Martinique include Saint-Denis, which competes with nearby Ajoupa-Bouillon as the town with the most flowers. Surfers usually head to Grand Rivière, an unspoiled fishing village on the northern tip of the island. The waves there are great for surfing but too strong for swimming. Some tourists visit Sainte-Marie to watch rum being made in the Rum Museum.

Saint-Pierre, in the northwest portion of the island, served as the capital of Martinique before the eruption of Mount Pelée. The city is often referred to as the Little Paris of the West Indies. It features the Musée Vulcanologique, with displays from the 1902 disaster, including petrified rice and blobs of molten nails. It also has the Musée Paul Gauguin, a shrine to the famous Postimpressionist painter.

Cities and Towns of St. Lucia

Located in the northwestern portion of St. Lucia is the capital city of Castries. It was named after Marechal de Castries, a French colonial minister who governed the island in the late 1700s. About 20,000 people live in the city today. Some don't consider Castries particularly pretty, with its modern concrete and functional architecture.

Castries has a history of burning down, with disasters occurring in 1796, 1812, 1927, and 1948. As with other island towns, the busiest place in Castries is the market. It is a confusing and colorful jumble of furniture, food, and straw bags.

The two fishing towns of Anse la Raye and Canaries lie to the south and are stopping points on the way to the town of Soufrière, one of the oldest settlements on the entire island. At Gros Islet, near the northern tip of the island, loud parties on Friday nights will sometimes last until the morning.

THE COMMUNITIES OF ST. VINCENT AND THE GRENADINES

About 26,000 people live in Kingstown, the capital of St. Vincent. It is an *eclectic* mixture of old colonial homes and modern suburbs. There is a fish market here where men slap fish of all sizes and shapes onto marble slabs. In the nearby market building, women sell their fruits and vegetables, wheeling and dealing with customers in loud voices. On the steep slopes of Kingstown Valley are the oldest botanical gardens in the Americas. Founded in the 1760s, they feature some of the island's most amazing greenery, trees, and flowers.

About 22 miles (35 km) from Kingstown lies Georgetown. Once a busy, bustling town, it is now quite run-down.

Dominating the entire northern end of St. Vincent is the Soufrière volcano. It has had quite an eventful history, with eruptions in 1718, 1812, 1902 (killing almost 2,000), 1971, and 1979.

The line of islands belonging to St. Vincent and called the Grenadines includes some 30 separate islands spread out over 80 miles (129 km). Bequia (pronounced BECK-way) is the largest. A very developed place, it is a popular shopping spot for tourists. Mustique, a modern resort for the rich and famous, is a company-owned island, managed by a group of millionaires. Tiny Canovan is home to about 800 people, primarily fishermen and farmers. Mayreau, population of about 180, has no cars, roads, or electricity. Tobago Cays, a set of five uninhabited islets, is the most secluded of all the Grenadines. Union Island, at 4 square miles (10 sq km), is home to about 3,000 and is a drop-off point for other islands because it has an airport. Petit St. Vincent, the southernmost of the islands, is a place where the rich go for seclusion and sunshine.

Three women carry metal pails of water while standing on the path overlooking their village on Canouan, one of the Grenadine islands.

St. George's, Grenada

The capital of Grenada, St. George's is a working port where cruise ships, cargo vessels, and yachts pull in and depart on a regular basis. Named after

A view of St. George's, the picturesque capital city of Grenada.

King George III, it is considered the loveliest harbor town in the entire Caribbean. Factories, churches, and sloping hillsides stacked with red-roofed homes glow at sunsets against the surrounding lush greenery. St. George's is divided into two sections: Carenage, the inner harbor, and the Esplanade, facing out to the Caribbean Sea. The two are linked by the 300-foot (483-meter) Sendall tunnel, built at the end of the 19th century.

The Carenage, the heart of the city, is home to the Grenada National Museum, which includes Arawak *petroglyphs* and the marble bathtub that once belonged to the French empress Josephine, who was born on Martinique. Several forts and churches galore can be found in the Carenage. In the Esplanade, or Bay Town, as it is sometimes called, are old warehouses, the fish market and main food market, an art gallery, and the original Fort

George. Several miles south of St. George's is the island's most popular beach, Grand Anse, where people enjoy several miles of white, soft sand and a row of hotels.

CARRIACOU AND PETIT MARTINIQUE

Carriacou and Petit Martinique, the only other two inhabited islands in the territory, are located about 15 miles (24 km) north of Grenada. Carriacou, with an area of about 13 square miles (34 sq km), is home to about 8,000 people. The people of the island are known for building boats and, unfortunately, for smuggling food and manufactured goods from cargo ships. Hillsborough is the only village on the small island, and it contains just two streets.

Petit Martinique, about 3 miles (5 km) east of Carriacou, is even smaller. About 1,000 people live there and they too specialize in building small boats.

TEXT-DEPENDENT QUESTIONS
1. What city is the capital of Dominica?
2. About how many people live in the city of Castries, St. Lucia?
3. What is the southernmost of Grenadine islands?

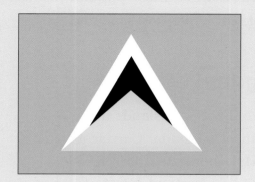

St. Lucia

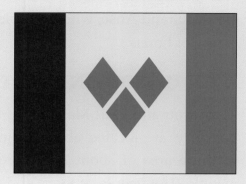

St. Vincent and the Grenadines

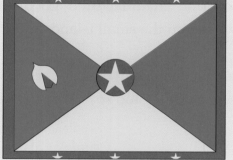

Grenada

Martinique

Dominica

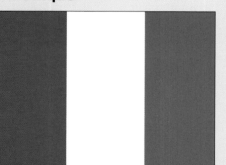

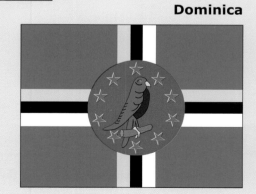

FESTIVALS OF THE WINDWARD ISLANDS

JANUARY

Carnival in Martinique

FEBRUARY

Independence Day in Grenada
Independence Day in St. Lucia

MARCH

Carnival in St. Lucia and Dominica

APRIL

Martinique Food Show

MAY

Jazz festival in St. Lucia

JUNE

Carnival or Vincy Mas in St. Vincent

JULY

Bastille Day in Martinique
Cultural Festival in Martinique
Domfesta in Dominica

AUGUST

Carnival in Grenada
Sailing Regatta in Grenada

OCTOBER

Independence Day in St. Vincent
Jounen Kweyol (Creole celebration) in St. Lucia and Dominica

NOVEMBER

Extempo in Grenada
St. Cecilia Day in St. Lucia
Independence Day in Dominica

DECEMBER

Nine Days Festival in St. Vincent
National Day in St. Lucia

Corn Pudding (Dominica)

2 15–oz. cans of creamed corn
2 qts. milk, or 10 oz. cream of coconut
1/2 lb. granulated sugar
2 oz. cornstarch
1 vanilla bean
2 oz. ground cinnamon

Directions:
1. With a blender, combine the creamed corn, cream of coconut and half the milk.
2. Pass through a medium mesh strainer; add the rest of the milk, sugar, and vanilla bean and bring to a boil.
3. Reduce to a simmer, add cinnamon, and cook gently for 10 minutes.
4. Dissolve cornstarch in a little of water and add.
5. When pudding is thickened, turn off heat at once, remove vanilla bean and pour the pudding into individual cups and dust with ground cinnamon. Do not refrigerate before serving.

Nutmeg Ice Cream (Grenada)

1-1/2 cups milk
1-1/2 cups heavy cream
3 large Eggs
3/4 cup sugar
1 tsp. freshly grated nutmeg
1/8 tsp. salt
1/4 tsp. vanilla

Directions:
1. In a saucepan, bring the milk and the cream just to a boil.
2. In a bowl, whisk together the eggs, sugar, nutmeg, salt, and vanilla.
3. Whisk 1/2 cup of the milk mixture into the egg mixture and whisk this into the remaining milk mixture.
4. Cook the custard over moderate heat, stirring constantly with a spatula until it registers 175°F on a candy thermometer.
5. Transfer the custard to a metal bowl set in a larger bowl of ice and cold water and stir it until it is cold. Freeze the custard.

Cod Fritters (Martinique)

8 oz. flour
1 glass water
1 pinch of baking soda
1 onion
1 clove of garlic
5 chives
dash of parsley
dash of thyme
dash of salt
dash of pepper
1/2 hot pepper
4 oz. cod
2 eggs
1 drop of vinegar

Directions:
1. Place the cod in cold water for a few hours, them bring to a boil for 30 minutes.
2. Whisk the flour and add water little by little to avoid lumps.
3. Let the cod cool, take the skin and ones off and then mince it thinly with the onion, garlic, chives, thyme, parsley, and hot pepper.
4. Season the batter to your taste and add egg yolks, vinegar and, just before cooking, the baking soda and egg whites stiffly beaten.
5. Dip the batter in very hot oil for about five minutes in small amounts.

Ground Provisions Medley (St. Lucia)

1/2 medium sized dasheen
2 sweet potatoes
1/4 sm. Breadfruit
4 grains green fig
2 grains of plantain
1 Tbsp. salt
1 large onion
2 Tbsp. butter
2 Tbsp. oil
2 cloves garlic
2 red peppers
2 green peppers
2 stalks celery
Chopped parsley as garnish

Directions:
1. Peel the ground provisions and put in a big pan of water with salt. Cover and boil for about 45 minutes to an hour until it is cooked and then let cool.
2. Put the butter, oil, and peppers in a large saucepan and fry over low heat, stirring constantly so the butter doesn't scorch.
3. When the ground provisions are cool, dice all of them into a large bowl. Pour the butter mixture over them, sprinkle the chopped parley over the top and serve warm.

Amerindian—a term for the indigenous peoples of North, Central, and South America, including the Caribbean islands, before the arrival of Europeans in the late 15th century.

cay—a low island or reef made from sand or coral.

civil liberty—the right of people to do or say things that are not illegal without being stopped or interrupted by the government.

conquistador—any one of the Spanish leaders of the conquest of the Americas in the 1500s.

Communism—a political system in which all resources, industries, and property are considered to be held in common by all the people, with government as the central authority responsible for controlling all economic and social activity.

coup d'état—the violent overthrow of an existing government by a small group.

deforestation—the action or process of clearing forests.

economic system—the production, distribution, and consumption of goods and services within a country.

ecotourism—a form of tourism in which resorts attempt to minimize the impact of visitors on the local environment, contribute to conserving habitats, and employ local people.

embargo—a government restriction or restraint on commerce, especially an order that prohibits trade with a particular nation.

exploit—to take advantage of something; to use something unfairly.

foreign aid—financial assistance given by one country to another.

free trade—trade based on the unrestricted exchange of goods, with tariffs (taxes) only used to create revenue, not keep out foreign goods.

hurricane—a very powerful and destructive storm, characterized by high winds and significant rainfall, that often occurs in the western Atlantic Ocean and the Caribbean Sea between June and November.

leeward—a side that is sheltered or away from the wind.

mestizo—a person of mixed Amerindian and European (typically Spanish) descent.

offshore banking—a term applied to banking transactions conducted between participants located outside of a country. Such transactions Some Caribbean countries have become known for this practice thanks to their banking laws.

plaza—the central open square at the center of colonial-era cities in Latin America.

plebiscite—a vote by which the people of an entire country express their opinion on a particular government or national policy.

population density—a measurement of the number of people living in a specific area, such a square mile or square kilometer.

pre-Columbian—referring to a time before the 1490s, when Christopher Columbus landed in the Americas.

regime—a period of rule by a particular government, especially one that is considered to be oppressive.

service industry—any business, organization, or profession that does work for a customer, but is not involved in manufacturing.

windward—the side or direction from which the wind is blowing.

In Your Opinion

Look up information about the U.S. invasion of Grenada on the Internet and in history textbooks. It was a controversial decision at the time. Why? Do you think President Reagan and the U.S. made the right decision to invade? Write a two-page report describing what happened and support your argument with details.

Film at Eleven

Research the Mount Pelée eruption and then write a news report as if you had been there and had witnessed what happened.

Art Time

Look up pictures and other information about the Soufrière volcano and then draw what it looks like, including details about its height and eruption history.

Cooking Time

Make a meal out of several of the recipes listed in this book (with parental permission and/or help). Write an evaluation of the dishes, including your family's responses to the food.

Just Imagine

Write a story about what it would be like to live on one of these islands. Pick whichever one you like best—even an uninhabited one. Include details about what your main character would do, eat, and enjoy in his or her free time. Read it to your parents or teacher.

Endangered List

Find out more information on the sisserou parrot found on the Windward Islands. Why is it endangered? What is being done about its endangered status? Prepare an oral report on what you find out.

Commercial Break

Imagine that you are writing an ad for a vacation to Dominica. You want to appeal to eco-tourists. What would you say? Write either a television commercial or a display ad for the newspaper.

A Poet Speaks

Look up some poetry by Derek Walcott and read it. Find your favorite poem and share it with someone.

You Are There

Imagine that you are a Carib Indian and you are being forced to leave your island by the British. What would you do? How would you feel? Write a story of the experience from a first-person perspective.

Make a List

Write down all the ways you think your life differs from that of a kid your age on one of the Windward Islands. Next, figure out if the positive differences outweigh the negative ones. Discuss the list with your parents or classmates and write a paragraph explaining why you would rather stay where you are or live on one of the Windward Islands.

1300	Carib Indians conquer the Arawaks on St. Vincent.
1493	Columbus visits Dominica and names it.
1498	Columbus visits St. Vincent; also sights and names Grenada.
1501	St. Lucia is sighted by Columbus.
1635	Martinique is settled by Pierre Belain d'Esnambuc.
1650	French settlers from Martinique establish a colony on Grenada and found the capital of St. George's.
1763	Dominica is ceded to Britain in Treaty of Paris.
1778	The French take back Dominica.
1783	Treaty of Versailles recognizes St. Vincent as a British colony; France cedes Grenada to Britain; slaves are brought to Grenada to work on plantations; Dominica is returned to Britain.
1812	First recorded eruption of Soufrière takes place on St. Vincent.
1814	France cedes St. Lucia to Britain following the Treaty of Paris.
1834	Slavery is abolished.
1902	The second eruption of Soufrière takes place on St. Vincent, killing 2000; Mount Pelée erupts on Martinique, killing 38,000.
1950	Grenada United Labour Party is founded.
1967	St. Lucia is granted internal self-government; Grenada is granted internal self-government.
1969	St. Vincent is granted internal self-government.
1974	Grenada is granted independence.

1978	Dominica is granted independence.
1979	St. Vincent is granted independence; St. Lucia is granted independence.
1983	The United States invades Grenada after Maurice Bishop is executed.
1985	Martinique is claimed as a territory of France.
1992	Derek Walcott from St. Lucia wins the Nobel Prize in literature.
1995	Keith Mitchell becomes prime minister of Grenada.
1997	Kenny Anthony becomes prime minister of St. Lucia in landslide election.
1999	Hurricane Lenny damages homes and plantations along the west coast of St. Vincent.
2000	James Mitchell resigns as prime minister of St. Vincent; Pierre Charles becomes new party leader in Dominica.
2002	An economic crisis in Dominica, and a government tax increase intended to help relieve the crisis, leads to protests in Roseau.
2004	In September, Hurricane Ivan tears through Grenada, killing 39 people and leaving more than 100,000 people homeless.
2007	Cricket World Cup matches are held on several Caribbean islands, including Grenada, St. Lucia, and St. Vincent.
2010	The Windward Islands Farmers Association says a prolonged dry spell has caused a significant decrease in the production and export of bananas.
2013	Floods and mudslides caused by unseasonable 2013 rainfall on St. Vincent cause substantial damage to homes and wipes out the banana crop.

Cheng, Pang Guek. *Grenada*. Tarrytown, N.Y.: Marshall Cavendish, 2000.

Furgang, Kathy. *Mount Pelee: The Deadliest Volcano Eruption of the Twentieth Century*. New York: Powerkids Press, 2001.

Heuman, Gad. *The Caribbean: A Brief History*. New York: Bloomsbury, 2014.

Keen, Benjamin, and Keith Haynes. *A History of Latin America*. Boston: Wadsworth Cengage Learning, 2013.

Pavlidis, Stephen J. *A Cruising Guide to the Windward Islands*. Port Washington, WI: Seaworthy Publications, 2005.

Sullivan, Lynne. *Martinique, Guadeloupe, Dominica and St. Lucia Alive!* Edison, N.J.: Hunter Publishing, 2000.

Travel Information

http://stlucianow.com/
http://www.martinique.org
http://www.grenadagrenadines.com/
http://www.discoversvg.com/
http://www.dominica.dm/

History and Geography

http://www.countryreports.org
  (Facts about all islands can be found here)

Economic and Political Information

https://www.cia.gov/library/publications/the-world-factbook/index.html
  (Facts about all islands can be found here)

Embassy of Grenada
1701 New Hampshire Ave., NW
Washington, DC 20009
Tel: 202-265-2561
Fax: 202-265-2468
Website: www.grenadaembassyusa.org
Email: embassy@grenadaembassyusa.org

Embassy of the Commonwealth of Dominica
3216 New Mexico Ave., NW
Washington, DC 20016
Tel: 202-364-6781
Fax: 202-364-6791
Email: Embdomdc@aol.com

**Embassy of Saint Vincent
and the Grenadines**
3216 New Mexico Ave., NW
Washington, DC 20016
Tel: 202-364-6730
Fax: 202-364-6736

Embassy of Saint Lucia
3216 New Mexico Ave., NW
Washington, DC 20016
Tel: 202-364-6792
Fax: 202-364-6723

Embassy of Martinique
4101 Reservoir Road, NW
Washington, DC 20007
Tel: 202-944-6000
Fax: 202-944-6166

CONTRIBUTORS

Senior Consulting Editor **James D. Henderson** is professor of international studies at Coastal Carolina University. He is the author of *Conservative Thought in Twentieth Century Latin America: The Ideals of Laureano Gómez* (1988; Spanish edition *Las ideas de Laureano Gómez* published in 1985); *When Colombia Bled: A History of the Violence in Tolima* (1985; Spanish edition *Cuando Colombia se desangró, una historia de la Violencia en metrópoli y provincia*, 1984); and coauthor of *A Reference Guide to Latin American History* (2000) and *Ten Notable Women of Latin America* (1978).

Mr. Henderson earned a bachelor's degree in history from Centenary College of Louisiana, and a master's degree in history from the University of Arizona. He then spent three years in the Peace Corps, serving in Colombia, before earning his doctorate in Latin American history in 1972 at Texas Christian University.

Tamra Orr lives in Portland, Oregon. She is the author of over a half-dozen nonfiction books for children and families. In her spare time, she enjoys reading and talking to her kids and husband. She says that they teach her something every day.